Fear Not

PRAYERS & PROMISES FOR Difficult Times

BroadStreet
PUBLISHING

Contents

Abandonment	4
Ability	6
Acceptance	8
Anxiety	10
Assurance	12
Authenticity	14
Beauty	16
Belief	18
Blessing	20
Boldness	22
Change	24
Comfort	26
Compassion	28
Composure	30
Confidence	32
Consolation	34
Contentment	36
Courage	38
Deliverance	40
Depression	42
Encouragement	44
Eternity	46
Faith	48
Faithfulness	50
Fear	52
Forgiveness	54
Freedom	56
Friendship	58
Goodness	60
Grace	62
Gratitude	64
Grief	66
Guidance	68
Health	70
Hope	72
Identity	74
Inspiration	76
Joy	78
Justice	80
Life	82
Loneliness	84
Loss	86
Love	88
Patience	90
Peace	92
Perseverance	94
Praise	96
Prayer	98
Promises	100
Protection	102
Provision	104
Purpose	106
Reconciliation	108
Relaxation	110
Reliability	112
Relief	114
Restoration	116
Reward	118
Safety	120
Salvation	122
Strength	124
Stress	126
Support	128
Trust	130
Truth	132
Understanding	134
Victory	136
Wholeness	138
Wisdom	140
Worry	142

Introduction

Everyone experiences difficult seasons in life. Loss, pain, anxiety, sickness, and frustration can lead to discouragement and sometimes a feeling of hopelessness.

Fear Not: Prayers & Promises for Difficult Times is a topically organized collection that guides you through themes of assurance, compassion, inspiration, purpose, and more. Encouraging Scriptures, heartfelt prayers, and prompting questions give you an opportunity to think more deeply about the hope found in God's Word.

By staying connected to God, and believing in his promises, you can live a fulfilling, blessed life. There is no place for fear in the calming peace of his presence. Take comfort in knowing that he cares deeply for you and he will always be with you.

Abandonment

"The LORD himself goes before you and will be with you;
he will never leave you nor forsake you."

DEUTERONOMY 31:8 NIV

The Lord loves justice and fairness;
he will never abandon his people.
They will be kept safe forever.

PSALM 37:28 TLB

God has said,
"I will never fail you. I will never abandon you."
So we can say with confidence,
"The LORD is my helper,
so I will have no fear."

HEBREWS 13:5-6 NLT

"I will not abandon you as orphans—
I will come to you."

JOHN 14:18 NLT

God, you say over and over in your Word that you will not leave me. Give me eyes to see you when I feel alone. Let my heart know your nearness when I cry out to you. You never turn away from those who need you, and oh, how I need you in this moment! I will cling to the truth that your ever-present help is at hand, especially when I've reached the end of my rope. Today, may the comfort of your presence melt away every fear and lead me into love.

Do you truly believe that God will never leave you?

Ability

"My grace is sufficient for you, for my power is made perfect in weakness." Therefore I will boast all the more gladly of my weaknesses, so that the power of Christ may rest upon me.

2 Corinthians 12:9 esv

After you have suffered for a little while, the God of all grace, who called you to His eternal glory in Christ, will Himself perfect, confirm, strengthen and establish you.

1 Peter 5:10 nasb

Take a new grip with your tired hands and strengthen your weak knees. Mark out a straight path for your feet so that those who are weak and lame will not fall but become strong.

Hebrews 12:12-13 nlt

We are not saying that we can do this work ourselves. It is God who makes us able to do all that we do.

2 Corinthians 3:5 ncv

Sometimes, Lord, I question your call on my life. I deeply desire to follow you and do great things in your name, but I don't trust my own humanity. Thank you for the numerous examples in the Bible of times you chose to use weak men and women to carry out your mission. Thank you for the times in my life when you've used me in spite of my shortcomings. May they serve as a reminder that true strength is only found in you. Thank you for having grace with my inabilities and granting me the ability to proceed with what you have called me to do.

Do you believe that God can make you able to do what he asks?

Acceptance

"The Father gives me the people who are mine.
Every one of them will come to me,
and I will always accept them."

JOHN 6:37 NCV

The LORD does not see as man sees; for man looks at the
outward appearance, but the LORD looks at the heart.

1 SAMUEL 16:7 NKJV

If God is for us, who can be against us?

ROMANS 8:31 ESV

Before he made the world, God chose us to be his very
own through what Christ would do for us; he decided
then to make us holy in his eyes, without a single fault—
we who stand before him covered with his love.

EPHESIANS 1:4 TLB

Father, sometimes when people act wrongly toward me,
I struggle to forgive them and let the grievance go. I know
you do not hold my sins against me but receive me in my
brokenness. Please give me the grace to likewise accept the
imperfection of others and treat them the way I have been
treated by you. Remind me, Lord, of the incredible price you
paid for me and also for them.

How does God's acceptance of you help
you to be more accepting of others?

Anxiety

Lord, you are my shield,
My wonderful God who gives me courage.
I can lie down and go to sleep, and I will wake up again,
Because the Lord gives me strength.
Thousands of troops may surround me,
but I am not afraid.

Psalm 3:3, 5-6 NCV

"Don't let your hearts be troubled. Trust in God, and
trust also in me."

John 14:1 NLT

Give all your worries to him,
because he cares about you.

1 Peter 5:7 NCV

I call out to the Lord when I'm in trouble,
and he answers me.

Psalm 120:1 NIRV

Lord, you know my heart and my every thought. You know when I sit and when I stand. You know my history and my future. There are no mysteries to you. When doubts and fears threaten to overwhelm my mind and body, be the peace that calms the storm. I will remember who you are: Defender, Savior, the Good Shepherd. You are my hope. I will trust in you, even when it takes everything inside of me to choose it. I will remember that though I cannot see the way out, you see it all so clearly and you are never overwhelmed. I trust you, God.

What steps can you take to be less anxious and more trusting?

Assurance

To him who is able to do immeasurably more than all we ask or imagine, according to his power that is at work within us, to him be glory...for ever and ever! Amen.

EPHESIANS 3:20–21 NIV

All of God's promises have been fulfilled in Christ with a resounding "Yes!"

2 CORINTHIANS 1:20 NLT

I go to bed and sleep in peace,
because, LORD, only you keep me safe.

PSALM 4:8 NCV

These things I have written to you who believe in the name of the Son of God, that you may know that you have eternal life, and that you may continue to believe in the name of the Son of God.

1 JOHN 5:13 NKJV

God, when all the worries of daily life engulf me, I begin to feel overwhelmed and anxious. When I change my focus and use your Word to light my path, my vision clears and my perspective accurately adjusts. I do not wish to use this as a reason to avoid life's problems, but I cling to the assurance that you are with me while I walk through them, each step of the way, no matter what.

How does believing God's promises cause you to feel reassured?

Authenticity

"Remember this: If you have a lofty opinion of yourself and seek to be honored, you will be humbled. But if you have a modest opinion of yourself and choose to humble yourself, you will be honored."

MATTHEW 23:12 TPT

What should be our proper response to God's marvelous mercies? I encourage you to surrender yourselves to God to be his sacred, living sacrifices. And live in holiness, experiencing all that delights his heart. For this becomes your genuine expression of worship. Stop imitating the ideals and opinions of the culture around you, but be inwardly transformed by the Holy Spirit through a total reformation of how you think. This will empower you to discern God's will as you live a beautiful life, satisfying and perfect in his eyes.

ROMANS 12:1–2 TPT

"From here on, worshiping the Father will not be a matter of the right place but with the right heart.

For God is a Spirit, and he longs to have sincere
worshipers who worship and adore him
in the realm of the Spirit and in truth."

JOHN 4:23–24 TPT

*God, I am painfully aware of the imbalance in our
relationship. There have been countless times when I was
unfaithful to you and you still remained devoted to me. I
do not pretend to be deserving of your love and loyalty, but
I accept them gratefully. You are not impressed by lofty,
religious airs, as I may fool myself into imagining. What you
ask me for is worship from a contrite heart, honestly aware of
my need for you. That is how I will come before you today.*

How do you see yourself? How do you
think God sees you?

Beauty

Your beauty should come from within you—
the beauty of a gentle and quiet spirit that will never be
destroyed and is very precious to God.

1 PETER 3:4 NCV

Hold on to wisdom and good sense.
Don't let them out of your sight.
They will give you life
and beauty like a necklace around your neck.
Then you will go your way in safety,
and you will not get hurt.

PROVERBS 3:21-23 NCV

She puts on strength and honor
as if they were her clothes.
She can laugh at the days that are coming.

PROVERBS 31:25 NIRV

I praise you because you made me
in an amazing and wonderful way.

What you have done is wonderful.
I know this very well.

PSALM 139:14 NCV

Lord, when I look at the abundance of diversity in the world around me, I remember that beauty comes in many forms. When you created me, you did it intentionally. Thank you that you made me unique and that beauty is so much more than skin-deep. Let beauty first grow in my heart, spilling out into the rest of my being. Wisdom and good sense make me beautiful to you, and they keep me safe from the troubles of the world. Help me to clothe myself with strength and honor as well, so I do not have to worry about what may come in this life. You are my confidence.

How does beauty look different to you
after reading these verses?

Belief

"For God so loved the world that he gave his one and only Son, that whoever believes in him shall not perish but have eternal life. For God did not send his Son into the world to condemn the world, but to save the world through him. Whoever believes in him is not condemned."

JOHN 3:16, 18 NIV

To all who did accept him and believe in him he gave the right to become children of God.

JOHN 1:12 NCV

Believe on the Lord Jesus Christ, and you will be saved.

ACTS 16:31 NKJV

"All things are possible to him who believes."

MARK 9:23 NASB

"Blessed are those who have not seen and yet have believed."

JOHN 20:29 ESV

Jesus, I believe that you are the Son of God. You came to earth as a human so that I could know what the Father is really like. Above all, you taught me what it means to love without condition. I believe you are still loving and kind, and I can trust you with my life. Thank you for the gift of knowing you. I pray that my belief would lead me into greater confidence in my relationship with you. Thank you that you are near and not distant. Whatever happens in the world around me, I believe that you remain constant.

How can you strengthen your belief in God?

Blessing

LORD, you bless those who do what is right.
Like a shield, your loving care keeps them safe.

PSALM 5:12 NIRV

Surely you have granted him unending blessings
and made him glad with the joy of your presence.

PSALM 21:6 NIV

"Even more blessed are all who hear the word of God
and put it into practice."

LUKE 11:28 NLT

Give praise to the God and Father of our Lord Jesus
Christ. He has blessed us with every spiritual blessing.
Those blessings come from the heavenly world. They
belong to us because we belong to Christ. God chose us to
belong to Christ before the world was created. He chose
us to be holy and without blame in his eyes. He loved us.

EPHESIANS 1:3-4 NIRV

*Even in the middle of difficulty and seasons of hardship,
everywhere I look, Father, I am confronted with your blessings.
Some of them seem incredible, while others I have adjusted
to perceiving as commonplace. The sun rises every morning
and I take it for granted, yet it is one of your wonderous
miracles nonetheless. Please give me fresh eyes to recognize the
countless blessings that surround me, so I may always be in
awe of you and never doubt your provision and protection.*

Which of God's blessings come to your
mind today?

Boldness

He proclaimed the kingdom of God
and taught about the Lord Jesus Christ—
with all boldness and without hindrance!

ACTS 28:31 NIV

If an army surrounds me, I will not be afraid.
If war breaks out, I will trust the LORD.

PSALM 27:3 NCV

Sinners run away even when no one is chasing them.
But those who do what is right are as bold as lions.

PROVERBS 28:1 NIRV

On the day I called you, you answered me.
You made me strong and brave.

PSALM 138:3 NCV

Let us come boldly to the throne of our gracious God.
There we will receive his mercy, and we will find grace to
help us when we need it most.

HEBREWS 4:16 NLT

Lord, in the middle of struggles and uncertainty, give me boldness so I can speak the truth in the moments that matter. My insecurities can cause a crippling timidity to overtake me, so help me see past myself and remember that my boldness stems from the assurance I have in you. Help me to not be intimidated by those who are stronger or smarter because you are more powerful and wise than anyone. It is on behalf of you and not myself that I step up and speak out.

Why is it sometimes hard to be bold?

Change

Look! I tell you this secret:
We will not all sleep in death,
but we will all be changed.

1 CORINTHIANS 15:51 NCV

He will take our weak mortal bodies and change them
into glorious bodies like his own, using the same power
with which he will bring everything under his control.

PHILIPPIANS 3:21 NLT

Jesus Christ is the same yesterday and today and forever.

HEBREWS 13:8 NIRV

I will not be afraid, because the LORD is with me.
People can't do anything to me.

PSALM 118:6 NCV

Lord, when change threatens to overwhelm me, help me to remember that change brings with it hope for better things ahead. When it feels as if the bottom has dropped out of life and I don't know what my future will look like, I know that I can trust in you. You stay the same forever, and there are no mysteries to you. You see and know every step of my journey. You know the end from the beginning and you are not surprised by anything. I trust in you, the unchanging one.

How do you handle change?

Comfort

"God's dwelling place is now among the people, and he
will dwell with them…. 'He will wipe every tear from
their eyes. There will be no more death' or mourning or
crying or pain."

<small>REVELATION 21:3–4 NIV</small>

May our Lord Jesus Christ himself and God our Father,
who loved us and by his grace gave us eternal comfort
and a wonderful hope, comfort you and strengthen you.

<small>2 THESSALONIANS 2:16–17 NLT</small>

Unless the LORD had helped me,
I would soon have settled in the silence of the grave.
I cried out, "I am slipping!"
but your unfailing love, O LORD, supported me.
When doubts filled my mind,
your comfort gave me renewed hope and cheer.

<small>PSALM 94:17–19 NLT</small>

I will give them a crown to replace their ashes,
and the oil of gladness to replace their sorrow,
and clothes of praise to replace their spirit of sadness.

ISAIAH 61:3 NCV

Worldly comforts are, at times, so enticing. But when true comfort is required, there is no substitute for the calm serenity your Holy Spirit brings to my soul. I try to liken it to the wind and the waves, but there is no explaining it, God, there is only experiencing it. I feel it in the worst moments of my life when you whisper to my heart, "It's going to be okay, my child, I have you."

Do you feel the comforting presence
of God today?

Compassion

When I am with those who are weak, I share their
weakness, for I want to bring the weak to Christ.
Yes, I try to find common ground with everyone,
doing everything I can to save some.

1 Corinthians 9:22 nlt

God, have mercy on me
according to your faithful love.
Because your love is so tender and kind,
wipe out my lawless acts.

Psalm 51:1 nirv

Praise be to the God and Father of our Lord Jesus Christ,
the Father of compassion and the God of all comfort.

2 Corinthians 1:3 niv

The Lord hears his people when they call to him for help.
He rescues them from all their troubles.

Psalm 34:17 nlt

Father, you see my suffering and my dejection, and you have compassion on me. You intervene on my behalf, forgive me, and renew me. You ask me to extend the same grace to others. May the compassion I have been given be the overflow that I pour out on others. The realization of your love toward me will fuel my grace toward those who may at times be difficult to love. They are as much in need of compassion as I am.

How can you be a more
compassionate person?

Composure

God is the one who saves me;
I will trust him and not be afraid.

ISAIAH 12:2 NCV

You will sleep like a baby, safe and sound—
your rest will be sweet and secure.
You will not be subject to terror, for it will not terrify you.
Nor will the disrespectful be able to push you aside,
because God is your confidence in times of crisis,
keeping your heart at rest in every situation.

· PROVERBS 3:24-26 TPT

Give your burdens to the LORD,
and he will take care of you.

PSALM 55:22 NLT

If people's thinking is controlled by the sinful self, there
is death. But if their thinking is controlled by the Spirit,
there is life and peace.

ROMANS 8:6 NCV

Make me like a tree with deep roots, God. When the worries of the world weigh me down, help me maintain my composure by being firmly rooted in you. Nothing is able to shake me when you are with me. Your Word promises that if I give you my burdens, you will take care of me, so I am choosing to do that today.

How can you remain steady when it feels like your world is crumbling around you?

Confidence

I can do everything through Christ,
who gives me strength.

PHILIPPIANS 4:13 NLT

Be my rock of refuge,
to which I can always go;
give the command to save me,
for you are my rock and my fortress....
For You have been my hope, Sovereign LORD,
my confidence since my youth.

PSALM 71:3, 5 NIV

Perfect, absolute peace surrounds those
whose imaginations are consumed with you;
they confidently trust in you.

ISAIAH 26:3 TPT

Do not throw away your confidence,
which has a great reward.

HEBREWS 10:35 NCV

God, your Word assures me that through you, I can do everything, yet so often my confidence wavers. Every challenge I have encountered, you have led me though. Your promise to me of being my hope and my confidence will never fail. Please help me to recall these times of victory in the middle of difficulties that make me feel overwhelmed or insecure. I have confidence knowing that you are with me always.

How do you find your confidence?

Consolation

You, O LORD, are a shield about me,
My glory, and the One who lifts my head.

PSALM 3:3 NASB

Blessed be the LORD,
Because He has heard the voice of my supplication.
The LORD is my strength and my shield;
My heart trusts in Him, and I am helped;
Therefore my heart exults,
And with my song I shall thank Him.

PSALM 28:6-7 NASB

He did rescue us from mortal danger, and he will rescue
us again. We have placed our confidence in him, and he
will continue to rescue us.

2 CORINTHIANS 1:10 NLT

The righteous person faces many troubles,
but the LORD comes to the rescue each time.

PSALM 34:19 NLT

In the darkest moments when words no longer comfort, your peace calms and encourages me. Your consolation can carry me through the worst of times when everything else falls short. Thank you for being my strength and my shield, God.

How do you feel you have been consoled by God in your moments of grief?

Contentment

To enjoy your work and to accept your lot in life—that is
indeed a gift from God. The person who does that will
not need to look back with sorrow on his past, for God
gives him joy.

ECCLESIASTES 5:20 TLB

I know what it is to be in need, and I know what it is to
have plenty. I have learned the secret of being content
in any and every situation, whether well fed or hungry,
whether living in plenty or in want. I can do all this
through him who gives me strength.

PHILIPPIANS 4:12-13 NIV

Those that the LORD has rescued will return.
They will enter Zion with singing;
everlasting joy will crown their heads.
Gladness and joy will overtake them,
and sorrow and sighing will flee away.

ISAIAH 35:10 NIV

God, I understand that the purpose of this season is not just to transition me into the next season. Regardless of what is coming or what I'm aiming at, you have a purpose for today. You have lessons you want to teach me and blessings you want to give me now. Please help me grow in contentment and appreciate what you have already done in my life especially when it is difficult to see what you are doing in the present moment.

How can you choose to be content with your life as it is right now?

Courage

Be strong in the Lord and in his mighty power.
Put on the full armor of God, so that you can
take your stand against the devil's schemes.

EPHESIANS 6:10-11 NIV

Be alert. Continue strong in the faith.
Have courage, and be strong.
Do everything in love.

1 CORINTHIANS 16:13-14 NCV

Even though I walk through the darkest valley,
I will not be afraid. You are with me.
Your shepherd's rod and staff comfort me.

PSALM 23:4 NIRV

"This is my command—be strong and courageous!
Do not be afraid or discouraged.
For the LORD your God is with you wherever you go."

JOSHUA 1:9 NLT

You came near when I called to you;
You said, "Don't be afraid."

LAMENTATIONS 3:57 NCV

Wherever I go, Father, you promise you'll be there. That means whatever I face I won't face alone because you are always with me. Please grant me courage to walk through everything that comes my way, knowing that you have already equipped me with all that I need to live a life of godliness and unrelenting faith.

When was the last time you asked God for courage?

Deliverance

I waited patiently for the Lord; he turned to me and heard my cry. He lifted me out of the slimy pit, out of the mud and mire; he set my feet on a rock and gave me a firm place to stand. He put a new song in my mouth, a hymn of praise to our God. Many will see and fear the Lord; and put their trust in him.

PSALM 40:1–3 NIV

Humble yourselves in the sight of the Lord, and He will lift you up.

JAMES 4:10 NKJV

My prayer is to you, O Lord.
At an acceptable time, O God,
in the abundance of your steadfast love
answer me in your saving faithfulness.
Deliver me from sinking in the mire;
let me be delivered from my enemies
and from the deep waters.

Answer me, O LORD, for your steadfast love is good;
according to your abundant mercy, turn to me.

PSALM 69:13-14, 16 ESV

God, you did not promise that I would be free from misfortune. In fact, your Word reveals that a righteous person is guaranteed to encounter trouble. Your promise to me is that you will come to my rescue and deliver me. Please deliver me from my fears today. I am not asking for an easy life or that you remove all problems from my path, but that you give me confidence in knowing that there is no trial so great that you won't deliver me from it.

Can you ask God for deliverance
from your fears?

Depression

Why am I so sad? Why am I so upset?
I should put my hope in God
and keep praising him.

PSALM 42:11 NCV

You, O LORD, are a shield about me, my glory,
and the lifter of my head.

PSALM 3:3 ESV

He has delivered us from the power of darkness and
conveyed us into the kingdom of the Son of His love.

COLOSSIANS 1:13 NKJV

"I am Yahweh, your mighty God!
I grip your right hand and won't let you go!
I whisper to you:
'Don't be afraid; I am here to help you!'"

ISAIAH 41:13 TPT

*Faithful Father, I need you to be the lifter of my head.
When darkness clouds my mind and settles over me like an
unwelcome haze, I know I cannot wish it away. You, God, are
my deliverer. I will choose to put my hope in you no matter
what I'm feeling. Please do the heavy lifting here, Lord. As I
choose you, do what only you can do. Let the light of your love
shine through the fog of despair and loneliness, bringing relief
and freedom. You are my only hope.*

Can you sense God's comfort and joy in the
middle of your sadness?

Encouragement

The LORD your God is with you;
the mighty One will save you.
He will rejoice over you.
You will rest in his love;
he will sing and be joyful about you.

ZEPHANIAH 3:17 NCV

Encourage one another daily,
as long as it is called "Today."

HEBREWS 3:13 NIV

Kind words are like honey—
sweet to the soul and healthy for the body.

PROVERBS 16:24 NLT

Be joyful. Grow to maturity.
Encourage each other.
Live in harmony and peace.
Then the God of love and peace will be with you.

2 CORINTHIANS 13:11 NLT

God, you told us that when we gather together in your name, you are with us. You said that when we encourage each other and live in harmony, you will be there. You are a God of peace, love, and joy! Show me ways today to extend that peace, love, and joy to others and be an encouragement to them. This, you tell me, will refresh my soul and bring health to my body. The way you created me to need others especially in difficult times is masterfully designed. Thank you for the encouragement you bring me through others.

How can you encourage someone today?

Eternity

We are citizens of heaven,
where the Lord Jesus Christ lives.
And we are eagerly waiting for him
to return as our Savior.

PHILIPPIANS 3:20 NLT

"If I go and prepare a place for you, I will come back and
take you to be with me that you also may be where I am."

JOHN 14:3 NIV

That will happen in a flash,
as quickly as you can wink an eye.
It will happen at the blast of the last trumpet.
Then the dead will be raised to live forever.
And we will be changed.

1 CORINTHIANS 15:52 NIRV

Surely your goodness and love will be with me all my life,
and I will live in the house of the LORD forever.

PSALM 23:6 NCV

I do not live for this life but for the hope of an eternal home with you. God, although I want to live intentionally and offer praise to you here on earth, I know that I was created for your kingdom and not simply this temporal existence. My treasures are not here, they are with you. My hopes and dreams are not wasted on present passing idols, they are focused forward to that "flash of an eye" when you come back for me. While I am here, help me to focus on the hope of eternity instead of on the difficult situations that seem to persist.

Can you view eternity with a hopeful, happy heart, fully trusting in a good God?

Faith

Through Christ you have come to trust in God. And you
have placed your faith and hope in God because he raised
Christ from the dead and gave him great glory.

1 PETER 1:21 NLT

"If you have faith as small as a mustard seed, it is enough.
You can say to this mountain,
'Move from here to there.'
And it will move.
Nothing will be impossible for you."

MATTHEW 17:20 NIRV

Since we have been made right in God's sight by faith,
we have peace with God because of what Jesus Christ our
Lord has done for us. Because of our faith, Christ has
brought us into this place of undeserved privilege where
we now stand, and we confidently and joyfully look
forward to sharing God's glory.

ROMANS 5:1–2 NLT

The important thing is faith—
the kind of faith that works through love.

GALATIANS 5:6 NCV

Faith is confidence in what we hope for and assurance
about what we do not see.

HEBREWS 11:1 NIV

*Since the beginning of time you have proven your faithfulness
to us, Father. Your goodness has never wavered and your
character is unchanged. I can confidently put my faith in you
because you have always been and always will be faithful
and true. Even when times are tough and situations are
difficult, what little faith I can offer you still accept, and you
can use it to move mountains. Even though I can't always see
what is coming, I know I can trust you.*

What helps increase your faith?

Faithfulness

Your lovingkindness, O LORD, extends to the heavens,
Your faithfulness reaches to the skies.

PSALM 36:5 NASB

The Lord is faithful, who will establish you and guard you
from the evil one.

2 THESSALONIANS 3:3 NKJV

LORD, you are my God;
I will exalt you and praise your name,
for in perfect faithfulness
you have done wonderful things,
things planned long ago.

ISAIAH 25:1 NIV

The word of the LORD is upright,
and all his work is done in faithfulness.

PSALM 33:4 ESV

Your faithfulness is what has established me. At times, I can become so distracted by my troubles and cares that I fail to realize how far you have already brought me. You have protected me from evil, released me from my sin, anointed me as your heir, and reserved for me a place in heaven with you. You have always remained true to your promises and I stand on those now in these trying times.

How have you seen the faithfulness of God played out in your life?

Fear

God gave us his Spirit. And the Spirit doesn't make us
weak and fearful. Instead, the Spirit gives us power and
love. He helps us control ourselves.

2 TIMOTHY 1:7 NIRV

The LORD is my light and my salvation—
whom shall I fear?
The LORD is the stronghold of my life—
of whom shall I be afraid?

PSALM 27:1 NIV

We can say with confidence, "The LORD is my helper,
so I will have no fear. What can mere people do to me?"

HEBREWS 13:6 NLT

When I am afraid, I will trust you.
I praise God for his word.
I trust God, so I am not afraid.
What can human beings do to me?

PSALM 56:3-4 NCV

The damage people and situations are able to inflict on me is severely limited because, God, you hold my heart. You are my light, my salvation, and the stronghold of my life. You are my helper, and you equip me with confidence to overcome my fears. Each and every fear I have, even the most hidden ones, you are aware of, and you will give me the tenacity to face them with power and in love.

What fears can you give to God right now?

Forgiveness

He is so rich in kindness and grace that he purchased our
freedom with the blood of his Son and forgave our sins.

Ephesians 1:7 NLT

As far as the east is from the west,
So far has He removed our transgressions from us.

Psalm 103:12 NASB

If we confess our sins, He is faithful and just to forgive us
our sins and to cleanse us from all unrighteousness.

1 John 1:9 NKJV

"Her sins—and they are many—have been forgiven,
so she has shown me much love. But a person who is
forgiven little shows only little love."

Luke 7:47 NLT

"If you forgive other people when they sin against you,
your heavenly Father will also forgive you."

Matthew 6:14 NIV

Father, I ask that you help me forgive those who have done me wrong. It is not a matter of whether or not they deserve forgiveness; I want to extend it because I was also guilty and you forgave me. My aim is to be like you. Please walk me through releasing my desire for justice, knowing that you are a just and loving God. You understand each situation far better than I could, and I can trust you to make all things right. Thank you for not holding my sins against me. Your forgiveness allows me to forgive others.

Is there someone who needs your forgiveness today?

Freedom

The Lord is the Spirit,
and where the Spirit of the Lord is,
there is freedom.

2 Corinthians 3:17 niv

My brothers and sisters, you were chosen to be free.
But don't use your freedom as an excuse to live under the
power of sin. Instead, serve one another in love.

Galatians 5:13 nirv

"If the Son sets you free, you are truly free."

John 8:36 nlt

We have freedom now, because Christ made us free.
So stand strong. Do not change and go back into the
slavery of the law.

Galatians 5:1 ncv

God, I live in freedom because I have accepted your forgiveness. I want to use this liberty to help others who are still trapped in bondage. I want them to understand that it is not on account of my merit that I walk in freedom, but only by your grace. The forgiveness I have been given drives me to do good, not for the notion that I could ever earn or repay your goodness, but as an outpouring of the gratefulness I feel each day as I walk in freedom.

How does it feel to be free from your sin?

Friendship

A friend loves you all the time,
and a brother helps in time of trouble.

PROVERBS 17:17 NCV

There are "friends" who destroy each other,
but a real friend sticks closer than a brother.

PROVERBS 18:24 NLT

"Greater love has no one than this: to lay down one's
life for one's friends. You are my friends if you do what
I command.... Instead, I have called you friends, for
everything that I learned from my Father I have made
known to you."

JOHN 15:13-15 NIV

"In everything, do to others what you would want them to
do to you."

MATTHEW 7:12 NIRV

There is nothing you wouldn't do for your friends, Lord. You modeled what true friendship looks like, and then lovingly instructed me to go and do likewise. Real, selfless friendship is not easy, but I have your example to follow. Thank you for the friends you have given me and the love they have shown me. Thank you for the ones who still stand with me through hard times. Thank you for the people in my life who don't just tell me what I want to hear but encourage me to continue drawing nearer to you.

What friends spur you on in your relationship with God?

Goodness

Everything God created is good, and nothing is to be
rejected if it is received with thanksgiving.

1 TIMOTHY 4:4 NIV

Taste and see that the LORD is good.
Oh, the joys of those who take refuge in him!

PSALM 34:8 NLT

I remain confident of this:
I will see the goodness of the LORD
in the land of the living.

PSALM 27:13 NIV

They will tell about the amazing things you do,
and I will tell how great you are.
They will remember your great goodness
and will sing about your fairness.

PSALM 145:6-7 NCV

*How can I begin to comprehend your goodness, God?
Everywhere I look I see your hand at work in my life. You
are my creator, Savior, and sustainer. You provide a refuge
for me to be safe. You offer forgiveness from sin through your
sacrifice, so I am pure enough to draw near to you. You
designed me for an eternal kingdom while still providing
for all my earthly needs. I can only just begin to recognize
the ways your goodness has reformed my life. Help me to
be aware of your goodness in the middle of testing times. I
want to continue to live with a grateful heart in spite of my
circumstances.*

Where do you see the goodness of God in
your life?

Grace

From his fullness we have all received, grace upon grace.

John 1:16 nrsv

God gives us even more grace,
as the Scripture says,
"God is against the proud,
but he gives grace to the humble."

James 4:6 ncv

Sin is no longer your master, for you no longer live
under the requirements of the law. Instead, you live
under the freedom of God's grace.

Romans 6:14 nlt

Christ gave each one of us the special gift of grace,
showing how generous he is.

Ephesians 4:7 ncv

Having been removed from the bondage of the law by your grace, I can now obey your commandments from a heart of love and gratitude, rather than as the joyless obligation of a servant. Your grace is my freedom. In humility, I will accept your grace and follow you every day of my life. I will enjoy our friendship, learn from your teachings, extend grace to others, and one day enter your kingdom. All these things I can do because, by your grace, I am your child and not merely a servant.

What does God's grace look like
in your life?

Gratitude

I have not stopped giving thanks for you, remembering
you in my prayers.

EPHESIANS 1:16 NIV

Giving thanks is a sacrifice that truly honors me.
If you keep to my path,
I will reveal to you the salvation of God.

PSALM 50:23 NLT

Rejoice always, pray continually,
give thanks in all circumstances;
for this is God's will for you in Christ Jesus.

1 THESSALONIANS 5:16–18 NIV

Give thanks as you enter the gates of his temple.
Give praise as you enter its courtyards.
Give thanks to him and praise his name.

PSALM 100:4 NIRV

God my Father, thank you for your lovingkindness toward
me. Thank you for the gift of family and friends. Thank you
that you have been faithful all my life. When I am struggling
to see any good, all it takes is stepping back and finding the
small, true things to see those glimpses of grace. I will practice
gratitude until it is as natural as breathing. Thank you for
this very moment I am in. Thank you for perspective. Thank
you for the warmth of the sunshine. Thank you that in spite of
hardship, you are still on the throne, and you still care for me.

What can you thank God for right now?

Grief

Those who sow in tears shall reap with shouts of joy.

PSALM 126:5 ESV

Let your steadfast love become my comfort
according to your promise to your servant.

PSALM 119:76 NRSV

"Come to me, all you who are weary and burdened, and I
will give you rest. Take my yoke upon you and learn from
me, for I am gentle and humble in heart, and you will
find rest for your souls."

MATTHEW 11:28-29 NIV

Every valley shall be raised up,
every mountain and hill made low;
the rough ground shall become level,
the rugged places a plain.

ISAIAH 40:4 NIV

I have experienced times of terrible grief, but you have always been faithful to walk with me through them. You are no stranger to grief, Father, and you console me like nothing else can. Furthermore, you have overcome grief. It is temporary and you are everlasting. There is coming a day when sorrow will end and there will be no more tears. Until that day comes, please continue to comfort me and allow me to lean on you for strength.

Do you ask God for help when you need his comfort?

Guidance

Guide me in your truth and teach me,
for you are God my Savior,
and my hope is in you all day long.

PSALM 25:5 NIV

I praise the LORD because he advises me.
Even at night, I feel his leading.
I keep the LORD before me always.
Because he is close by my side,
I will not be hurt.

PSALM 16:7-8 NCV

We can make our plans,
but the LORD determines our steps.

PROVERBS 16:9 NLT

Those who are led by the Spirit of God
are children of God.

ROMANS 8:14 NIRV

God, sometimes I get irritated when things don't go the way I plan. You are the one directing my steps, and that knowledge gives me peace that surpasses the disruptions. You determine my path. I want to be led by your Spirit. Guide me in your ways and grant me wisdom to listen and learn. Do not allow me to become so stuck in my ways that I lose sight of your guidance.

Is there anything God can help guide you in today?

Health

The world and its desires pass away,
but whoever does the will of God lives forever.

1 JOHN 2:17 NIV

Don't be wise in your own eyes.
Have respect for the Lord and avoid evil.
That will bring health to your body.
It will make your bones strong.

PROVERBS 3:7-8 NIRV

I will never forget your commandments,
for by them you give me life.

PSALM 119:93 NLT

A happy heart is like good medicine,
but a broken spirit drains your strength.

PROVERBS 17:22 NCV

You are a masterful designer, God, and you created our bodies to need you in order to truly thrive. Your Word says that respecting you and obeying your commandments will help me experience health and strength. A joyful disposition not only uplifts me emotionally, but it also brings wellness to my physical body. Thank you, Lord, for the ways you have provided for me both physically and emotionally. Thank you for the joy and the health you have given me. Thank you that in the end I know everything will be made new.

What healing are you believing God for right now?

Hope

The LORD is good to those whose hope is in him,
to the one who seeks him.

LAMENTATIONS 3:25 NIV

Hope will never bring us shame. That's because God's
love has poured into our hearts. This happened through
the Holy Spirit, who has been given to us.

ROMANS 5:5 NIRV

The LORD's delight is in those who fear him,
those who put their hope in his unfailing love.

PSALM 147:11 NLT

God has given both his promise and his oath. These two
things are unchangeable because it is impossible for God to
lie. Therefore, we who have fled to him for refuge can have
great confidence as we hold to the hope that lies before us.
This hope is a strong and trustworthy anchor for our souls.
It leads us through the curtain into God's inner sanctuary.

HEBREWS 6:18-19 NLT

Father, I can hope in things unseen because I know that I am seen. You see me, listen to me, and love me. Because you are good, I can put my hope in you and seek you with all my heart. Because you have given me your Spirit and poured out your love on me, I have assurance that my hope will never be put to shame. Because your delight is in me, I hope for all your promises and have confidence in them because your love for me never fails.

Knowing that God always hears you,
what can you be hopeful for?

Identity

See how very much our Father loves us, for he calls us his children, and that is what we are! But the people who belong to this world don't recognize that we are God's children because they don't know him. Dear friends, we are already God's children, but he has not yet shown us what we will be like when Christ appears. But we do know that we will be like him, for we will see him as he really is.

1 JOHN 3:1-2 NLT

Do everything without grumbling or arguing, so that you may become blameless and pure, "children of God without fault in a warped and crooked generation." Then you will shine among them like stars in the sky as you hold firmly to the word of life.

PHILIPPIANS 2:14-16 NIV

I have been crucified with Christ;
and it is no longer I who live,
but Christ lives in me;

and the life which I now live in the flesh
I live by faith in the Son of God,
who loved me and gave Himself up for me.

GALATIANS 2:20 NASB

Loving God, thank you that you have called me your child. I get all the benefits of being your very own—that is almost unfathomable! Oh, how I want to be more like you. Thank you that you are changing me into your image even through the hard and dry seasons. When I don't know anything else, I remember that you have called me your child. You didn't call me an acquaintance, servant, or distant relative. Father, let my heart be rooted in this close relationship, knowing that you care for me. Shepherd me and teach me to be like you.

Who do you think God really sees when he looks at you?

Inspiration

The precepts of the LORD are right,
giving joy to the heart.
The commands of the LORD are radiant,
giving light to the eyes.

PSALM 19:8 NIV

Your laws are my treasure;
they are my heart's delight.

PSALM 119:111 NLT

The whole Bible was given to us by inspiration from
God and is useful to teach us what is true and to make us
realize what is wrong in our lives; it straightens us out
and helps us do what is right.

2 TIMOTHY 3:16 TLB

Father, you inspire me by your life, your Word, and your creation. When I spend time with you, I am inspired to love you deeper. Reading the Scriptures encourages me to press forward toward my goal of knowing you more. Everywhere I look I am surrounded by testimonies of your beauty and creativity which makes me want to pursue truth and uncover your treasures. You inspire me to see things the way you do. Even when times are difficult, I trust that you have the bigger picture in mind and you continue to be with me through it all.

How do you find inspiration?

Joy

May the God of hope fill you with all joy and peace as you
trust in him, so that you may overflow with hope by the
power of the Holy Spirit.

ROMANS 15:13 NIV

"Don't be sad, because the joy of the LORD
will make you strong."

NEHEMIAH 8:10 NCV

The LORD is my strength and shield.
I trust him with all my heart.
He helps me, and my heart is filled with joy.
I burst out in songs of thanksgiving.

PSALM 28:7 NLT

Always be joyful because you belong to the Lord.
I will say it again. Be joyful!

PHILIPPIANS 4:4 NIRV

Your joy is more than mere happiness, Lord, it is everlasting sustenance. Joy that comes from you fills me with peace, strength, and thankfulness. It is not a moment of fleeting satisfaction, but an enduring force that sustains me regardless of my difficult circumstances. God, I am so grateful that your joy is not dependent on my situation like worldly pleasures are, but it is a gift that you freely give to those who fear and follow you.

What is one truly joyful moment you've had recently?

Justice

He will not break the bruised reed, nor quench the dimly
burning flame. He will encourage the fainthearted, those
tempted to despair. He will see full justice given to all
who have been wronged.

ISAIAH 42:3 TLB

Beloved, do not avenge yourselves, but rather give place
to wrath; for it is written, "Vengeance is Mine, I will
repay," says the Lord.

ROMANS 12:19 NKJV

He will not judge by appearance, false evidence,
or hearsay, but will defend the poor and the exploited.
He will rule against the wicked who oppress them. For he
will be clothed with fairness and with truth.

ISAIAH 11:3–5 TLB

He did not retaliate when he was insulted, nor threaten
revenge when he suffered. He left his case in the hands
of God, who always judges fairly.

1 PETER 2:23 NLT

The wrongs of this world can seem overwhelming and I yearn for your justice, God. Help me to trust your omniscience and your justice. You are the Judge, not me. Your justice is perfectly executed, coupled with your mercy. Mine is flawed and biased. I can forgive and move on. Today, I will not seek vengeance for myself but will submit everything to you and follow your example. You are more aware than anyone of the condition of the world, and you have a perfect plan in place.

Can you leave justice in God's hands?

Life

All praise to God, the Father of our Lord Jesus Christ.
It is by his great mercy that we have been born again,
because God raised Jesus Christ from the dead. Now we
live with great expectation.

1 PETER 1:3 NLT

That faith and that knowledge come from the hope for life
forever, which God promised to us before time began.

TITUS 1:2 NCV

"I am the way and the truth and the life.
No one comes to the Father except through me."

JOHN 14:6 NIRV

The Word gave life to everything that was created,
and his life brought light to everyone.

JOHN 1:4 NLT

You gave me life. Then, you saved my life with your own blood. As if that were not miraculous enough, you gave my life meaning and purpose. You have richly blessed me and have offered me eternal life. I don't want to squander this gift or your sacrifice. Rather, I want to live my life to the fullest extent and bring you glory even when it means going through pain and struggles. Please guide me in big opportunities and also in the mundane day-to-day tasks so my whole life honors you.

What is your favorite part of life?

Loneliness

"Teach them to obey everything that I have taught you,
and I will be with you always,
even until the end of this age."

MATTHEW 28:20 NCV

The LORD is near to all who call on him,
yes, to all who call on him in truth.

PSALM 145:18 NLT

Even if my father and mother abandon me,
the LORD will hold me close.

PSALM 27:10 NLT

"Be strong and courageous.
Do not be afraid or terrified because of them,
for the LORD your God goes with you;
he will never leave you nor forsake you."

DEUTERONOMY 31:6 NIV

There is nowhere I can go that you will not go with me. You promise to always be near me and to answer when I call to you. Even if my own parents or my closest friends were to abandon me, you never will. You have broken the clutch loneliness had on my life and have become my best friend. Thank you for surrounding me with your presence and walking with me through all my trials and failures. Your constant nearness brings me great comfort.

When you feel lonely, can you turn to God and ask him to surround you with his presence?

Loss

Those who sow in tears shall reap with shouts of joy.

PSALM 126:5 ESV

Let your steadfast love become my comfort
according to your promise to your servant.

PSALM 119:76 NRSV

Every valley shall be raised up,
every mountain and hill made low;
the rough ground shall become level,
the rugged places a plain.

ISAIAH 40:4 NIV

LORD, have mercy, because I am in misery.
My eyes are weak from so much crying,
and my whole being is tired from grief.
In my distress, I said,
"God cannot see me!"
But you heard my prayer
when I cried out to you for help.

PSALM 31:9, 22 NCV

God, in my life I have endured times of immense loss, but that is not where my story ends. You do not leave me in the valley. I will rise again and, leaning on you, make my way up to the mountain top. It's steep and I stumble at times, but I know I cannot sit in the empty feeling of loss forever. There is too much that you want to give me for me to fixate on what has been taken. You are my worth—the One who fills my empty cup.

Do you ask God for help when you need his comfort?

Love

Three things will last forever—
faith, hope, and love—
and the greatest of these is love.

1 CORINTHIANS 13:13 NLT

LORD, you are good. You are forgiving.
You are full of love for all who call out to you.

PSALM 86:5 NIRV

Where God's love is, there is no fear,
because God's perfect love drives out fear.
It is punishment that makes a person fear,
so love is not made perfect in the person who fears.

1 JOHN 4:18 NCV

Fill us with your love every morning.
Then we will sing and rejoice all our lives.

PSALM 90:14 NCV

Let love and faithfulness never leave you;
bind them around your neck,
write them on the tablet of your heart.

PROVERBS 3:3 NIV

Your love, Lord, is everlasting! It is superior to faith, hope, and even the tongues of men and angels. Fill me with your love every morning so I can spend every day praising you and loving others. Your love gives me strength, puts joy in my heart, and casts out my fears. I want to share it with everyone I know especially when they are experiencing difficulty. Help me to love like you do.

How does the love of God in your life help you to love others?

Patience

Warn those who are lazy.
Encourage those who are timid.
Take tender care of those who are weak.
Be patient with everyone.

1 Thessalonians 5:14 NLT

Be like those who through faith and patience
will receive what God has promised.

Hebrews 6:12 NCV

Be completely humble and gentle;
be patient, bearing with one another in love.

Ephesians 4:2 NIV

Anyone who is patient has great understanding.
But anyone who gets angry quickly shows how foolish
they are.

Proverbs 14:29 NIRV

Patience can teach me many things, God. In fact, you tell me that I receive your promises by way of my faith and through exercising patience. Alternatively, when I act in hasty anger and am easily set off, I show everyone that I am foolish. I cannot see what you see, and I do not always understand what people are going through. It is best to listen to what you have said and have patience with everyone. Help me to also be patient with situations that aren't going the way I want them to. I know you will bring good out of every situation because I trust in you.

How can you show more patience
in your life?

Peace

"I have told you these things, so that you can have peace
because of me. In this world you will have trouble. But be
encouraged! I have won the battle over the world."

JOHN 16:33 NIRV

The LORD gives his people strength.
The LORD blesses them with peace.

PSALM 29:11 NLT

May the Lord of peace himself give you peace at all times
and in every way. The Lord be with all of you.

2 THESSALONIANS 3:16 NIV

"I am leaving you with a gift—peace of mind and heart.
And the peace I give is a gift the world cannot give.
So don't be troubled or afraid."

JOHN 14:27 NLT

Father, in a world filled with turmoil and uncertainty, you offer peace. This true and prevailing peace can only be found in you. The world does not possess it and cannot offer it. I cannot earn it or learn it. It is a gift and I can only choose to receive it. Your peace is far greater than the world's troubles because you are far greater than the world. Thank you for leaving me your peace so I don't need to live in fear or confusion anymore.

What does peace look like for you?

Perseverance

In a race all the runners run.
But only one gets the prize.
You know that, don't you?
So run in a way that will get you the prize.

1 CORINTHIANS 9:24-25 NIRV

I have tried hard to find you—
don't let me wander from your commands.

PSALM 119:10 NLT

I have fought the good fight, I have finished the race,
I have kept the faith.

2 TIMOTHY 4:7 NCV

Let us not become weary in doing good, for at the proper
time we will reap a harvest if we do not give up.

GALATIANS 6:9 NIV

God, when Moses' arms were tired, you sent others to hold them up. Through his obedience, you granted the army victory. At times, I feel so exhausted, but I know that you are holding me and helping me persevere. You have sent others to help me along and I know that I do not need to fight alone. Doing good often requires the harder path, but it is the road I am committed to taking. I will persevere in this race because I find my rest and my refreshment in you. In faith, I will run and not lose heart.

What do you feel God is calling you to persevere in right now?

Praise

Sing to the Lord a new song,
his praise from the ends of the earth,
you who go down to the sea,
and all that is in it, you islands,
and all who live in them.

Isaiah 42:10 niv

Praise the Lord from the skies.
Praise him high above the earth.
Praise him, all you angels.
Praise him, all you armies of heaven.
Praise him, sun and moon.
Praise him, all you shining stars.
Praise him, highest heavens
and you waters above the sky.
Let them praise the Lord,
because they were created by his command.

Psalm 148:1-5 ncv

God chose you to be his people. You are royal priests. You are a holy nation. You are God's special treasure. You are all these things so that you can give him praise. God brought you out of darkness into his wonderful light.

1 PETER 2:9 NIRV

God, I praise you because of how wonderful and powerful you are. You made me in your image and saved my life from the pit of death. You are worthy of all praise and I will never stop being amazed by all the glorious things you have done. I will not make my life about me because that is an empty existence. You give me purpose and fullness, and I will praise you for that today and every day. Thank you for the opportunity to approach you in worship because it is what I was created to do.

What is something specific you can praise God for today?

Prayer

LORD, in the morning you hear my voice.

In the morning I pray to you.

I wait for you in hope.

PSALM 5:3 NIRV

Never stop praying.

1 THESSALONIANS 5:17 NIRV

The LORD does not listen to the wicked,

but he hears the prayers of those who do right.

PROVERBS 15:29 NCV

Come, let us bow down in worship,

let us kneel before the LORD our Maker.

PSALM 95:6 NIV

When you pray, go away by yourself, shut the door

behind you, and pray to your Father in private.

Then your Father, who sees everything, will reward you.

MATTHEW 6:6 NLT

I love coming to you in prayer, Father. It astounds me that I can speak to you and you listen. Please listen to my prayers today as I recognize your greatness, thank you for your blessings, and ask you for your help. Through prayer, I can worship you. Through prayer, I can acknowledge the mighty things you have done in my life. Through prayer I can bring you all my fears, my tears, my regrets, and my requests. I never want to stop praying, God.

What can you pray about right now?

Promises

His divine power has granted to us everything pertaining
to life and godliness, through the true knowledge of Him
who called us by His own glory and excellence.

2 PETER 1:3-4 NASB

Your promises have been thoroughly tested,
and your servant loves them.
My eyes stay open through the watches of the night,
that I may meditate on your promises.

PSALM 119:140, 148 NIV

The LORD always keeps his promises;
he is gracious in all he does.

PSALM 145:13 NLT

All the promises of God in Him are Yes, and in Him
Amen, to the glory of God through us.

2 CORINTHIANS 1:20 NKJV

If it weren't for your promises, I would be too weak to endure until the end. You offer strength through your promises of help and restoration for the journey. You give relief from grief and an eternity with you in the end. You do not require blind obedience but have a history of fulfilled promises as far back as history dates. Furthermore, you have revealed your promises for the end of the age, and you have not hidden it from me. I only need to trust you and your promises.

Which promises of God help you see hope in your current situation?

Protection

My God is my rock. I can run to him for safety.
He is my shield and my saving strength,
my defender and my place of safety.
The LORD saves me from those who want to harm me.

2 SAMUEL 22:3 NCV

The LORD keeps you from all harm
and watches over your life.
The LORD keeps watch over you as you come and go,
both now and forever.

PSALM 121:7-8 NLT

The LORD is good, a refuge in times of trouble. He cares
for those who trust in him.

NAHUM 1:7 NIV

We are pushed hard from all sides. But we are not beaten
down. We are bewildered. But that doesn't make us lose
hope. Others make us suffer. But God does not desert us.
We are knocked down. But we are not knocked out.

2 CORINTHIANS 4:8-9 NIRV

God, there is no force as mighty as you. I know that I can surrender myself to your caring and capable hands. I do not need to anguish over self-protection because if you are for me there is nothing that can come against me. You are the God of the miraculous and you have always protected your children. There is nothing I need to be afraid of. Your protection covers me from every kind of evil and I trust you for that now.

How hard is it for you to lay down your battle plan and let God be your protector?

Provision

All scripture is inspired by God and is useful for
teaching, for reproof, for correction, and for training in
righteousness, so that everyone who belongs to God may
be proficient, equipped for every good work.

2 TIMOTHY 3:16–17 NRSV

May he give you the power to accomplish all the good
things your faith prompts you to do.

2 THESSALONIANS 1:11 NLT

We are God's handiwork, created in Christ Jesus to do
good works, which God prepared in advance for us to do.

EPHESIANS 2:10 NIV

"Seek the Kingdom of God above all else,
and he will give you everything you need.
So don't be afraid, little flock.
For it gives your Father great happiness
to give you the Kingdom."

LUKE 12:31-32 NLT

God, there is nothing that you have called me to that you won't also provide for. At times, the task of following you can seem too difficult and I feel like I am lacking in crucial areas. However, then I remember your promises to provide for everything I need to follow you. Your perfect provision includes the wisdom, compassion, and resources necessary for the calling you have placed on my life. Thank you for the assurance that you will continue to provide for me in the middle of difficult seasons. I trust you, God.

How have you seen God provide
for you lately?

Purpose

You have been raised up with Christ.
So think about things that are in heaven.
That is where Christ is.
He is sitting at God's right hand.

COLOSSIANS 3:1 NIRV

We know that in all things God works for the good of
those who love him, who have been called according to
his purpose.

ROMANS 8:28 NIV

My child, pay attention to my words;
listen closely to what I say.
Don't ever forget my words;
keep them always in mind.

PROVERBS 4:20-21 NCV

It is God who works in you to will and to act in order to
fulfill his good purpose.

PHILIPPIANS 2:13 NIV

I am in awe and humbled when I think of how you created me for a special purpose within your universal plan. Thank you for the opportunity to follow you and serve you—to fulfill the purpose you've placed on my life. Thank you for raising me up with Christ, from death into life, for a role in your kingdom. I look to you to continue to fulfill your purpose in me in spite of the obstacles I face and the difficulties that show up along the way. Your perfect plan is not thwarted by earthly mishaps.

How do you feel when you think about God having a special purpose for your life?

Reconciliation

We are made right with God by placing our faith in
Jesus Christ. And this is true for everyone who believes,
no matter who we are. For everyone has sinned; we
all fall short of God's glorious standard. Yet God, with
undeserved kindness, declares that we are righteous. He
did this through Christ Jesus when he freed us from the
penalty for our sins.

ROMANS 3:22–24, NLT

You were separate from Christ...foreigners to the
covenants of the promise, without hope and without God
in the world. But now in Christ Jesus you who once were
far away have been brought near by the blood of Christ.

EPHESIANS 2:12–13 NIV

We have stopped evaluating others from a human point
of view. At one time we thought of Christ merely from
a human point of view. How differently we know him
now! This means that anyone who belongs to Christ has
become a new person. The old life is gone; a new life has

begun! And all of this is a gift from God, who brought us back to himself through Christ. And God has given us this task of reconciling people to him.

2 CORINTHIANS 5:16–18 NLT

Father, my sin used to separate me from you, but you reconciled our broken relationship by paying the price for my sin and reclaiming me from the grip of death. In you, I have been made new, and this complete reconciliation has secured me a place in your family. I want to play an integral part in the lives of others and help them also reconcile their relationships with you. Show me how I can do this especially in the middle of trying circumstances.

Can you believe God for reconciliation in your relationships?

Relaxation

Blessed is the one who trusts in the Lord,
whose confidence is in him.
They will be like a tree planted by the water
that sends out its roots by the stream.
It does not fear when heat comes;
its leaves are always green.
It has no worries in a year of drought
and never fails to bear fruit.

JEREMIAH 17:7–8 NIV

Those who love me, I will deliver;
I will protect those who know my name.
When they call to me, I will answer them;
I will be with them in trouble,
I will rescue them and honor them.

PSALM 91:14-15 NRSV

Father, it can be difficult for me to relax and unwind at times. Life seems so hectic and I struggle to find spare time to sit with you and be at peace in your company. Even though you promise rest for the weary, I often overlook your offer and attempt to find my own way through this maze called life. Please remind me to trust you and to believe that you will take care of me. Help me look to you first for the rest that my body needs and to make it a priority in my life.

How can you practice relaxing in God's presence?

Reliability

"All people are like grass. All their glory is like the flowers in the field. The grass dries up. The flowers fall to the ground. But the word of the LORD lasts forever."

1 PETER 1:24-25 NIRV

Every good action and every perfect gift is from God. These good gifts come down from the Creator of the sun, moon, and stars, who does not change like their shifting shadows.

JAMES 1:17 NCV

He will give eternal life to those who keep on doing good, seeking after the glory and honor and immortality that God offers.

ROMANS 2:7 NLT

You are near, LORD,
and all your commands are true.
Long ago I learned from your statutes
that you established them to last forever.

PSALM 119:151-152 NIV

God, thank you that you don't make up your mind about something one day and change it the next. Your Word, your every intention, is firmer than the strongest foundations on earth. You do not get caught in a web of lies because you never lie. Thank you that what you say you will do. I trust you to be the same God who carried me through my darkest hours in these hard moments. I trust that you are not leaving me to my own devices; no pit of despair will swallow me up. You have been a God who cares, and you will always follow through. I trust you!

How does it make you feel knowing you can rely on God for everything?

Relief

"I am the Alpha and the Omega—the Beginning and the End. To all who are thirsty I will give freely from the springs of the water of life."

REVELATION 21:6 NLT

I prayed to the LORD, and he answered me.
He freed me from all my fears.
Those who look to him for help will be radiant with joy.

PSALM 34:4–5 NLT

If you will humble yourselves under the mighty hand of God, in his good time he will lift you up.

1 PETER 5:6 TLB

The Spirit helps us in our weakness. We do not know what we ought to pray for, but the Spirit himself intercedes for us through wordless groans. And he who searches our hearts knows the mind of the Spirit, because the Spirit intercedes for God's people in accordance with the will of God.

ROMANS 8:26–27 NIV

God, my soul is so anxious because of the burdens I choose to carry, but you extend rest and relief to me. Let me learn from you, Lord, and take up your yoke because you are gentle and humble. You answer my prayers, release me from fear, and fill me with joy. Your relief is like a fresh spring that lifts my spirit and calms my anxious mind.

What relief do you need from God in your current situation?

Restoration

He has saved us and called us to a holy life—
not because of anything we have done
but because of his own purpose and grace.

2 TIMOTHY 1:9 NIV

"Let us praise the Lord, the God of Israel,
because he has come to help his people
and has given them freedom.
He has given us a powerful Savior."

LUKE 1:68-69 NCV

We can boldly enter heaven's Most Holy Place because of
the blood of Jesus. By his death, Jesus opened a new and
life-giving way through the curtain into the Most Holy
Place. And since we have a great High Priest who rules
over God's house, let us go right into the presence of God
with sincere hearts fully trusting him.

HEBREWS 10:19—22 NLT

Jesus, since you paid for my sins with your own life, my life has been restored. You saved me because I could not save myself. You took what was dead and filled me with joy, peace, love, purpose, and bravery. The restoration powers of your grace have set me free to walk right up to you and into your Holy Place, which I previously would never dare enter because I was stained with sin. Thank you for restoring my life and inviting me into your presence.

Have you experienced the power of
restoration in your life?

Reward

Work willingly at whatever you do, as though you were working for the Lord rather than for people. Remember that the Lord will give you an inheritance as your reward, and that the Master you are serving is Christ.

COLOSSIANS 3:23-24 NLT

"Love your enemies, do good to them, and lend to them without expecting to get anything back. Then your reward will be great, and you will be children of the Most High, because he is kind to the ungrateful and wicked."

LUKE 6:35 NIV

Even if you suffer for doing what is right,
God will reward you for it.

1 PETER 3:14 NLT

Without faith it is impossible to please God. Those who come to God must believe that he exists. And they must believe that he rewards those who look to him.

HEBREWS 11:6 NIRV

God, your Word says that you are kind to people even when they are ungrateful and wicked. Help me to be like you, even when my diligent attempts seem to go unnoticed or unappreciated. You even promise to reward my diligence and my faith. When coworkers, family, friends, or just life's situations are difficult, I can remember that it is really you who I am serving. When all my hard work goes unacknowledged, I remember that you are my reward.

How does it make you feel knowing that God will reward you for your diligence?

Safety

The LORD also will be a refuge for the oppressed,
A refuge in times of trouble.
Those who know Your name will put their trust in You;
For You, LORD, have not forsaken those who seek You.

PSALM 9:9–10 NKJV

I call to you from the ends of the earth when I am afraid.
Carry me away to a high mountain.
You have been my protection,
like a strong tower against my enemies.

PSALM 61:2-3 NCV

"Don't be afraid of anyone,
because I am with you to protect you," says the LORD.

JEREMIAH 1:8 NCV

I look to my left and right
to see if there is anyone who will help,
but there's no one who takes notice of me.
I have no hope of escape,

and no one cares whether I live or die.
So I cried out to you, Lord, my only hiding place.
You're all I have, my only hope in this life,
my last chance for help.

PSALM 142:4-5 TPT

Fear has no voice next to you, Father. I know that when I am with you, I am safe. You provide safety from my enemies and assurance that I am never alone. In times of trouble, you are right there guarding me. When nobody else is around to help me, you are beside me ready to guide me. Thank you for always keeping me safe and close to you.

Do you feel safe when you think about God being near you?

Salvation

"This is how God loved the world: He gave his one and only Son, so that everyone who believes in him will not perish but have eternal life."

JOHN 3:16 NLT

The wages of sin is death,
but the gift of God is eternal life
in Christ Jesus our Lord.

ROMANS 6:23 NIV

God's grace has saved you because of your faith in Christ.
Your salvation doesn't come from anything you do.
It is God's gift.

EPHESIANS 2:8 NIRV

If you openly declare that Jesus is Lord and believe in
your heart that God raised him from the dead,
you will be saved.

ROMANS 10:9 NLT

There was a time when I had no hope for the future because I had sinned and could not approach you. I did not qualify for entrance into your kingdom because I was imperfect and couldn't bring my filth into your presence. Darkness does not approach the light. You saw me in the wretched state I was in, loved me, and offered me salvation by paying for my sins yourself. Your salvation is the greatest gift I have ever received! Thank you.

How do you respond to the message
of salvation?

Strength

God is our refuge and strength,
an ever-present help in trouble.

PSALM 46:1-3 NIV

The Lord is faithful;
he will strengthen you and guard you
from the evil one.

2 THESSALONIANS 3:3 NIRV

Don't be afraid, for I am with you.
Don't be discouraged, for I am your God.
I will strengthen you and help you.
I will hold you up with my victorious right hand.

ISAIAH 41:10 NLT

LORD, don't be far away.
You are my strength;
hurry to help me.

PSALM 22:19 NCV

The LORD protects those who truly believe....
All you who put your hope in the LORD
be strong and brave.

PSALM 31:23-24 NCV

Just as you gave David strength to conquer Goliath, please give me the strength to stand up against anything that defies you. There are a lot of evil forces that I am not strong enough to defeat, but you are stronger than them all. There is nothing that can stand against you, and you have put your strength in me. When I feel weak and insignificant, you take me by the hand and lead me into victory. I will not be discouraged because I know you are faithful.

What makes you feel strong?

Stress

Praise the LORD, my soul;
all my inmost being, praise his holy name.
Praise the LORD, my soul,
and forget not all his benefits—
who forgives all your sins
and heals all your diseases,
who redeems your life from the pit
and crowns you with love and compassion,
who satisfies your desires with good things
so that your youth is renewed like the eagle's.

PSALM 103:1-5 NIV

Commit your actions to the LORD.
and your plans will succeed.

PROVERBS 16:3 NLT

As pressure and stress bear down on me,
I find joy in your commands.

PSALM 119:143 NLT

As soon as the aim of my day becomes about me and my accomplishments, stress is invited in. Stress is needless if I have truly committed my plans and their results to you, God, because you will be the one who allows them to succeed or fail. I can till, plant, and water all day, but only you can cause a plant to grow. Sometimes I lose sight and get caught up chasing my end goals, and then I succumb to consequential stressful situations. Help me remember that you bring the increase and I can trust you with the results.

When was the last time you were able to let go of stress and just sit with God?

Support

Whom have I in heaven but you?
And earth has nothing I desire besides you.
My flesh and my heart may fail,
but God is the strength of my heart
and my portion forever.

PSALM 73:25–26 NIV

The LORD is near to the brokenhearted
and saves the crushed in spirit.

PSALM 34:18 ESV

You, God, see the trouble of the afflicted;
you consider their grief and take it in hand.
The victims commit themselves to you;
you are the helper of the fatherless.

PSALM 10:14 NIV

You are my hiding place;
You shall preserve me from trouble;
You shall surround me with songs of deliverance.

PSALM 32:7 NKJV

Sometimes my grief becomes too much to bear, and too much for others to bear as well. I feel as if the weight of it will crush me. Those are the moments when you intervene. Your Word says that you are near to the brokenhearted, you see the afflicted, you are the helper of the fatherless, and you will never forget the needy. You are not overwhelmed or disinterested in my anguish. In fact, it is where you dwell! My problems are not too big for you. You have taken my grief in your hand and have offered me a hiding place in you. You have given me hope.

When do you feel the most supported by God?

Trust

Those who know the LORD trust him,
because he will not leave those who come to him.

PSALM 9:10 NCV

I trust in you, LORD. I say, "You are my God."
My whole life is in your hands.
Save me from the hands of my enemies.
Save me from those who are chasing me.

PSALM 31:14-15 NIV

Yes, the LORD is for me; he will help me.
I will look in triumph at those who hate me.
It is better to take refuge in the LORD
than to trust in people.

PSALM 118:7-8 NLT

Take delight in the LORD,
and he will give you your heart's desires.
Commit everything you do to the LORD.
Trust him, and he will help you.

PSALM 37:4-5 NLT

My confidence in you, Lord, is rooted in your proven goodness and faithfulness stretched across all of history. Never in all of time has there been a more trustworthy testimony. You did not have to prove yourself to me, but you did and you continue to. Whenever I call on you, you answer. When I am faced with problems, you help me navigate them. In the instances you ask me to step out in faith and trust you, I find myself safely guarded by you the whole way through. I know I can securely put my trust in you.

How do you know that God is trustworthy?

Truth

"When he, the Spirit of truth, comes,
he will guide you into all the truth."

JOHN 16:13 NIV

The very essence of your words is truth;
all your just regulations will stand forever.

PSALM 119:160 NLT

"If you abide in My word, you are My disciples indeed.
And you shall know the truth, and the truth shall make
you free."

JOHN 8:31-32 NKJV

Teach me your way, O LORD, that I may walk in your truth;
unite my heart to fear your name.

PSALM 86:11 ESV

We will remain strong and always sincere in our love
as we express the truth.

EPHESIANS 4:15 TPT

God, you are the Spirit of truth, and if I am your child then I am also a child of truth. When faced with the temptation to be dishonest, I will remember that it is by your truth that I am set free. Help me to live honestly in the light. I pray that I learn to fear you more than the consequences of telling the truth. Your truth will always reign supreme and I want to walk in the same way you do.

What steps can you take to be more truthful in your everyday life?

Understanding

Understanding is like a fountain of life
to those who have it.

PROVERBS 16:22 NIRV

The teaching of your word gives light,
so even the simple can understand.

PSALM 119:130 NLT

Give me understanding,
so that I may keep your law and obey it with all my heart.

PSALM 119:34 NIV

Those who love your teachings will find true peace,
and nothing will defeat them.

PSALM 119:165 NCV

Don't act thoughtlessly,
but understand what the Lord wants you to do.

EPHESIANS 5:17 NLT

God, rather than acting foolishly in ignorance, help me to understand. I pray that every day I will grow in understanding as I read your teachings and keep your Word in my heart. Show me what you want me to do in these moments that are so difficult. Help me understand your Word so I can obey it. I do not need to be a scholar to follow you because you say even the simple can understand. Help me to retain what I have learned so I can live for you and share it with others.

How do you seek to understand God's will each day?

Victory

You can prepare a horse for the day of battle.
But the power to win comes from the LORD.

PROVERBS 21:31 NIRV

Every child of God defeats this evil world,
and we achieve this victory through our faith.

1 JOHN 5:4 NLT

Say to the anxious and fearful,
"Be strong and never afraid.
Look, here comes your God!
He is breaking through to give you victory!
He comes to avenge your enemies.
With divine retribution he comes to save you!"

ISAIAH 35:4 TPT

"The LORD your God is the one who goes with you to fight
for you against your enemies to give you victory."

DEUTERONOMY 20:4 NIV

*As a mighty leader and an omnipotent God, you have
already promised me victory over death. The end of my story
concludes in triumph and an everlasting life with you. You
have defeated the world and, so, I defeat it by having faith
in you. As I address the present battles faced every day, I can
have confidence knowing that you go with me and will help me
emerge victorious. The power to overcome is found in you alone.*

You win with Jesus in your life! Can you
think of the last victory you experienced?

Wholeness

He will take our weak mortal bodies and change them
into glorious bodies like his own, using the same power
with which he will bring everything under his control.

PHILIPPIANS 3:21 NLT

For you who fear my name, the sun of righteousness
shall rise with healing in its wings.

MALACHI 4:2 ESV

Celebrate with praises the God and Father of our Lord
Jesus Christ, who has shown us his extravagant mercy.
For his fountain of mercy has given us a new life—we are
reborn to experience a living, energetic hope through
the resurrection of Jesus Christ from the dead. We are
reborn into a perfect inheritance that can never perish,
never be defiled, and never diminish. It is promised
and preserved forever in the heavenly realm for you!
Through our faith, the mighty power of God constantly
guards us until our full salvation is ready to be revealed
in the last time.

1 PETER 1:3–5 TPT

God, my body is breaking down and I recognize this every day. Thank you that my hope is not in myself or my mortal body. Thank you that you bring healing and wholeness. Your mercy grants me new life and one day I will be reborn. This life and all of its splendors will break down and perish, but within the new life that you offer, I will experience what it is like to truly be whole. This is the reality that will remain forever.

How does understanding eternal wholeness benefit you in this life?

Wisdom

Wisdom will come into your mind,
and knowledge will be pleasing to you.
Good sense will protect you;
understanding will guard you
It will keep you from the wicked,
from those whose words are bad.

PROVERBS 2:10-12 NCV

Wisdom and money can get you almost anything,
but only wisdom can save your life.

ECCLESIASTES 7:12 NLT

If any of you needs wisdom, you should ask God for it.
He will give it to you. God gives freely to everyone
and doesn't find fault.

JAMES 1:5 NIRV

My brothers and sisters, I am sure that you are full of
goodness. I know that you have all the knowledge you
need and that you are able to teach each other.

ROMANS 15:14 NCV

The wisdom which comes from you will protect me from following foolish whims and ideas. When others set traps for me and try to get me to fall, wisdom will save me from the snares. Your wisdom is far superior to knowledge or money because it is true understanding that you have given me. If I ever need wisdom, you freely give it when I ask you for it. Please continue to help me make wise choices as I follow you through trials and difficulties.

How can you use God's wisdom to make better choices?

Worry

Turn your worries over to the LORD.
He will keep you going.
He will never let godly people be shaken.

PSALM 55:22 NIRV

"Who of you by worrying
can add a single hour to your life?"

LUKE 12:25 NIV

Worry weighs a person down;
an encouraging word cheers a person up.

PROVERBS 12:25 NLT

Do not worry about anything, but pray and ask God for everything you need, always giving thanks. And God's peace, which is so great we cannot understand it, will keep your hearts and minds in Christ Jesus.

PHILIPPIANS 4:6-7 NCV

God, you know how easily worries can overtake my mind. You know how overwhelmed my heart can get at the thought of everything that could go wrong. I don't want to be weighed down by worry; I give it over to you, God! I'm taking what energy I have and, with thanks, asking for all I need. When worry threatens to shut down my gratefulness and skew my view of life, gently turn me and I will hand them over to you. Thank you for faithfully keeping me going. I trust you for your provision in these areas.

What worries can you hand over
to God today?

BroadStreet Publishing Group, LLC.
Savage, Minnesota USA
Broadstreetpublishing.com

Fear Not: Prayers & Promises for Difficult Times

© 2020 by BroadStreet Publishing

978-1-4245-6184-1 (hardcover)
978-1-4245-6181-0 (ebook)

Design by Chris Garborg | garborgdesign.com
Compiled and edited by Michelle Winger | literallyprecise.com

Printed in China.

20 21 22 23 24 25 26   7 6 5 4 3 2 1

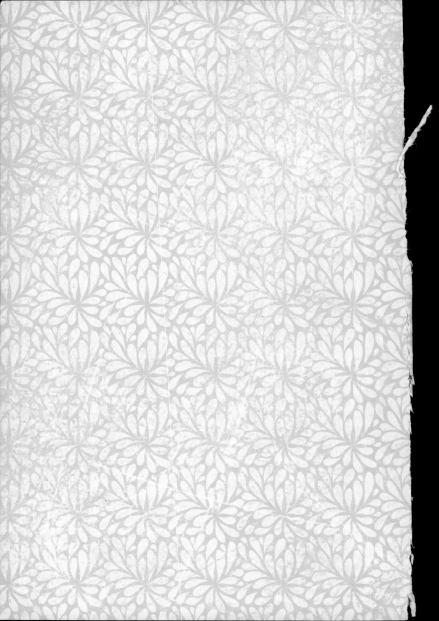